AVIANS OF MOURNING

poems by

Kate McCarroll Moore

Finishing Line Press
Georgetown, Kentucky

AVIANS OF MOURNING

Copyright © 2020 by Kate McCarroll Moore
ISBN 978-1-64662-280-1 First Edition
All rights reserved under International and Pan-American Copyright Conventions. No part of this book may be reproduced in any manner whatsoever without written permission from the publisher, except in the case of brief quotations embodied in critical articles and reviews.

ACKNOWLEDGMENTS

Thank you to Amy Ludwig VanDerwater, whose April 2018 poetry challenge, 1 subject 30 ways, inspired these bird poems

A big thank you to Paul Corman Roberts and the San Francisco Creative Writing Institute for the space and guidance that helped me find the narrative thread that links these poems

Special thanks to Helen Macdonald, whose transformative memoir *H is for Hawk* appeared in my hands at just the right moment

Publisher: Leah Maines
Editor: Christen Kincaid
Cover Art: Maren S. Smith
Author Photo: Nina Pomeroy Photography
Cover Design: Elizabeth Maines McCleavy

Order online: www.finishinglinepress.com
also available on amazon.com

Author inquiries and mail orders:
Finishing Line Press
P. O. Box 1626
Georgetown, Kentucky 40324
U. S. A.

Table of Contents

Memories Made of Air .... 1.

Empty .... 2.

Transplant .... 4.

Benediction .... 5.

Winter Conversation .... 6.

Through the Eyes of a Hawk .... 7.

Storm Warning .... 8.

Solitude .... 9.

Skylight .... 10.

Keening .... 11.

Beckoned .... 12.

Cleaning the Garage .... 14.

speak easy .... 15.

Tossed from the Nest .... 16.

Postscript/Unspoken .... 17.

Lake Luzerne, 1939 .... 18.

Escape .... 19.

A little bird told me .... 20.

Birdmanmac .... 21.

Over Dublin .... 22.

Grief .... 23.

A suburbanite ventures out, alone .... 24.

*This chapbook is dedicated to the memory of
Walter J. (aka Birdmanmac)*

"*...everything comes from something that came before,
which was once nothing.*"
Tommy Orange, *There There*

MEMORIES MADE OF AIR

So many memories appear, rising out of thin air.
Today I passed by a tree, heavy with orange berries
and my father suddenly appeared
leading me down the driveway
pointing to the laden branches,
this, he said, is mountain ash.

I was five, and he was a young man
on the cusp of everything yet to be
in his brush cut and plaid shirt
knower of trees and birds and history

He comes to me now in other moments
a song, a smell, the taste of beer
an internet story about milkman days
transports me back to the time
we went away for a week
and the milkman left two bottles on the front step
where they boiled in the Buffalo heat and exploded
sending white streams rushing down the front steps
till they soured and became two rivers of ants

My father in his undershirt
aiming the hose at the mess
whistling along to Nat King Cole
roll out those lazy hazy crazy days of summer
you'll wish that summer could always be here

Empty

Childhood days
made of long grey
hours drag
until
emerging from the gloom
he appears
whistling soft and low,
holding a box
that he sets down
gently
on the linoleum
pulls back the lid
like a magician
ta-da
revealing a squirming
shaking
ball of fur and wet nose
a desperate kind of love

The pup must feel it too
his frantic whining
and grateful nuzzling
burrowing into me
for hours on end
we can't leave each other alone

too wild, untamed
I should have listened when they told me to stop
let him rest

But I couldn't
wouldn't leave him alone
held on too tight for too long

I yelped when he bit my face
he yelped too
scooted under the couch
shaking and whimpering
childhood daze
a desperate kind of heartbreak
promises made, promises broken
the magician returns
gathers his equipment
first love carted away
in that same cardboard box
a disappearing act
ta-da

TRANSPLANT

At the end of summer
at the end of childhood
I dig up a sapling
from the woods behind our house
carry it home gently, cradling it like a baby
dig a shallow hole
in the new-mown lawn
dig with fervor
as the sun goes down

transplant, replant
metaphor in the making
little tree takes root
grows tall, then taller still
learns to commune
with birds and sky

Benediction

I learned to love the life-giving energy of earth from him
sun-burned Sundays spent on our knees
in the garden
digging bare-handed
gentling the roots
into safe spaces
patting dirt into tender brown mounds
sprinkling water as benediction

wiping rivulets of sweat from brows
broken nails on soil-crusted hands
we breathe in the moment
silent, reverent as we listen to a choir of songbirds
and the distant preaching of a crow

Winter Conversation

Time is running out
my father said last night
his words dropped with regret
into our casual conversation about the weather
It's the hard, inevitable truth
that lives in every moment,
propels us forward
with such urgency and denial
as if we could outrun the clock

On my walk today
I imagine
this neighborhood
a thousand years from now
tourists scavenging for a shard of glass
a remnant of this time

They'll piece together what they can of us
All of this means so much

and nothing at all

Through the Eyes of a Hawk

That patient hawk watching from the lightpole
messenger from the other side
this is the year that my father died.

This is the year that I put pen to paper
Bird scratch across the empty pages
Trying to capture a lifetime
then, oh,
the great unknown.

I wake to the smell of coffee
and the realization
again
you are no longer of this world.

I write down memories
I say your name
I study birds in the morning sky
in the hope that I can keep you alive.

Already you are fading
disappearing
day turns to deep dark night
my brother asks for signs
I only ask for answers.

Storm Warning

The birds understand
how today the sky
is a thick grey blanket
rippling in slow waves
releasing the unmistakable smell of *about to rain*

they were here this morning
singing among the roses
serenading with sunshine songs until
cautioned by the wind
they pack their belongings
to take a little daytrip

Me? I'm not so wind-tuned.
There I sat as the sky changed,
lost, deep in the pages of my book
splattered with raindrops
listening for birds no longer there

Solitude

Sky, the color of steel
more winter than spring
releases a torrent of rain
to pound on the roof
and remind me
of sorrows past

Rain pounding on the roof

I am all alone

Shadows of the past
grow distant
memories of other days
blur
into this here and now
a moment marked
by rain that won't stop
falling

Skylight

sudden shock of moon
overpowers a just darkened sky
this October night

insistent
through closed shutter slats
no denying its pull
heart rising with the fall

I cannot sleep

The moon will be here, always, still
permanent fixture
in this transitory life

Keening

Awakened from clouded dreams
who are these ghosts?
such keening
echoes through the house
cutting through the night
faces fading fast
memories dissolve
disappear
while I wander darkened hallways
heart pounding
in rhythm with Banshee wails
there must be life
beyond this darkness

Beckoned

Penny found
on the ground today
caught in a grate
at the base
of this city tree
where
it beckoned

so, stooping low
awkwardly balancing
beside sidewalk trash
and a flock of sooty pigeons
driven by instinct
or superstition
hoping for a bit of luck
determined to pocket it
before the rain falls

I hear his voice again
singing *pennies from heaven*
as the family gathered 'round
singing with new-found strength
you'll find your fortune fallin'
as he was passing from this world
into the next, singing
that's life I guess

the song dies out
as the wind starts up
and the rain begins to fall
a penny sent from beyond
wedged there, beneath the tree
stubborn copper, taunting me
unaware that I am
incapable of giving up
caught in a downpour
pawing the dirt
determined
to pry it loose
hold it tight
so I can be on my way

Cleaning the Garage

We start with a plan
move everything to one side
go through it box by box
make a pile of stuff to save
a pile to throw away
a pile for Goodwill
we're working together
remembering
working up a sweat

a mountain grows between us

a heap of soft scuffed baby shoes,
grandma's dishes, yellowed, chipped
now discarded
their stories lost
beneath the photographs and cards
love letters
bound together, aged and torn
pages once held tight
in an unlined hand

Every single thing I hold
whispers its story to me
but you
whistling along to Van Morrison
pushing your broom
across the littered floor
and laughing
unable to hear the song of our past
pulsing through the garage

speak easy

she was only six
when she sailed across an ocean
and came ashore to this new life
nearly drowning in words
a gurgling confusion of sound
swirling and eddying, constant

in school she learned to forget
the words that once named
the objects of her Sicilian life
she learned a new language then
through osmosis and necessity
      (her mother did not)

she learned to forget
how to answer her mother
who married at fourteen
left her island home
three children at her side
on a ship that rocked for days upon days
over stormy seas

she learned to forget
how to see her mother
who wandered the streets of her new city
nearly drowning in words
a gurgling confusion of sound
swirling and eddying, constant

her mother, alone and adrift,
dreaming of home
in a language all her own

Tossed from the Nest

The first time
I rescued a bird
I was eight years old
playing tag in Joey Hughes' yard

I stopped when he yelled freeze
looked down at my feet
and there, beside my scuffed Keds
a nearly naked bird

in that moment
everything froze
while I gathered
shoebox
tissue pillow
eyedropper
me

In my mind, the bird took rest and sustenance
grew feathers
learned to fly
brought its chicks to meet me
the girl who saved a life

Instead, despite my nursing
and desperate prayers
a different fate, life lesson learned
my father's steady hand, my shaking shoulders
his words resounding
        nothing you could have done
        happens every day
        other mouths to feed
        only the strong survive

Postscript/Unspoken

Do you remember that moment?
I was living in the city with that boy.
The one you hated.
(By the way, you were right about him)
I remember.

One particular day, I came home to a dark apartment.
Nothing to eat. I scraped together some change from the bottom of my bag, his coat pocket, the dark recesses of the Goodwill couch. It was dark, the rain coming down in loud brown sheets of sorrow. I walked to the corner market, cursing the rain and him. The fluorescent aisles were eerily empty. I rounded a corner to low voices. Two men talking. One of them was you, Daddy. There you stood, a salesman in a raincoat and fedora dripping rain. So out of place—both of us. Our eyes met.

Even now, my heart leaps, my throat catches. Your eyes meet mine, for a moment only. Silence. Sorrow. I turn away. The moment becomes the moment. Unspoken.

Postscript: If I'd left five minutes later, if there'd been enough to eat, if it wasn't raining, would the moment have been? Hard to say. Would the moment become the moment that became the moment I grew strong? Silence. Sorrow. Regret.
The strength to walk away.
The sense to leave.

Lake Luzerne, 1939

At twelve, he begged his father
to take in a game
just the two of them
lakeside
watching the pitcher warm up
this perfect day unfolding

A fast ball
the crack of the bat
ringing in his ears
and someone calling his name

His brother
caught in deep water
struggling to stay afloat
called out to him,
his voice carried on the wind

Their mother,
aproned behind the kitchen door
daydreaming and
whistling an old song,
heard the screams too late

Dark clouds rolled in
as they pulled his brother from the water
lifeless

A father gone deaf, a mother grown silent
a house of grief and blame

If only…
This would be their family story

ESCAPE

Grandpa walked out of the nursing home
wandered a mile away
stood on the corner,
spinning around
Which way is home?

Just like the little brown bird
that showed up this morning
hopping frantically
under desks
beneath tables
over extension cords and power cords
strewn like snakes
across the carpeted landscape
confused and confounded
—a little brown wren
pacing frantically
looking for a way out,
trying to find his way home

A little bird told me

When I was 16
my boyfriend bought me a parrot
and a cage to keep him in
I wanted a lovebird

I bought a 45 at Woolworths
played that record day and night
guaranteed to teach caged birds
to talk
Hello, baby, want a kiss?
Hello, baby, want a kiss?

He pulled his feathers out
one by one
refused to speak
barked like a dog
Still, I didn't understand
the misery of not being allowed to fly.

Birdmanmac

He would have turned 90 today
had he lived another year
his body, tinned ashes
buried beneath a tree, close to home
soothed now by wind
and soaring birds

We called him Birdmanmac
forever trying to outsmart squirrels
who hung from feeders, unafraid

One winter a hawk landed in the pear tree
outside his window
sat there staring steadily for hours
brothers in the fight against the enemy

Today we drove to see an eagle's nest
perched atop a redwood
watched the birds puff and preen
soon, they will send an eaglet out exploring

a year from now they'll return
same nest, same tree

Over Dublin

Something changes, coming in over Dublin
over the sea, over the green, so green
the air is charged
electric air, pounding heart
palpable, visceral
impossible to put into words
just a feeling
THE feeling…
sensation of home

Home.

I am here, in the place they left
driven out by famine, propelled by hope
their blood runs through me and recognizes home

Home.

In the morning
I get up early
walk to the corner coffee shop
buy an Irish Times
order tea
sit at a corner table and pretend to read the news
I'm imagining this kind of life

Home.

You have the map of Ireland on your face
they said when I was growing up.
I'll take you home again, Kathleen
my father sang
he sang *tura lura lural*
that's an Irish lullaby

GRIEF

But now my father had died.
Hold tight.
Hold tight.
The words on the page stung.
Something far away
something too familiar.

Suddenly
this memoir in my hands—
love and bereavement tangled,
laid open, raw and bare.

A late-night phone call.
My father had died.
Right then.
A moment earlier, he was himself
old and tired, but alive
in the world
and then he was not.

Hold tight.
I closed the book.
Stared into the yellow eyes of the hawk before me.

A suburbanite ventures out, alone

She rides the moving stairs to the platform
eleven minutes till the next train comes

Echoes of his voice in her head
litany of dos and don'ts

*Pay attention to your surroundings,
don't take your phone out*

*Be careful,
don't get lost in your book…*

That book, the one about a real life lived in squalor on a mountaintop
preparing for the end of days

A Pygmalion story, a transformation
Did it really happen like this?

She says it did. Does that make it true?
Memories are so complicated.

Remember that story about the Challenger explosion?
A professor gathered his students in the hours after and recorded
what they'd seen and heard.

Flash forward, eighteen months later, every story had changed.
False certainty, that's what they call these flashbulb memories.

She's thinking of that now as she closes her book
Looks to the man asleep in the next seat, how did he end up here?

Thinks of it again as she walks along Market,
trying not to see what's underneath the blanket,

what's shivering beneath the plastic bag,
what's shuffling along beside her, hand outstretched

Moving now with purpose. Don't think about it. Don't think.
Right on Turk Street. Right on Taylor.

Pay attention to your surroundings, don't take your phone out
Be careful, don't get lost inside your head…

She's moving in the wrong direction.
What if she came all this way and can't find it? What if she's lost?

Turns around,
defiant.

Crosses the street.
Turns around again.

Crosses again.
A vibration, then a disembodied voice

You have arrived.
The street is deserted. The door is locked.

Bella J. McCarroll

Kate McCarroll Moore is a collector of stories, discarded objects, and memories. She is a mentor teacher, book coach, and staff developer who served three terms as the Poet Laureate for the City of San Ramon. Kate holds a Doctorate in Educational Leadership for Social Justice and she uses her passion for poetry to promote kindness, empathy, and connection. She was an education columnist for several years and has published poems in numerous journals and anthologies. She is currently working on a community storytelling project and writing a poetry memoir. This is her first chapbook. Kate is grateful for her East Coast roots, and loves living with her husband in northern California where the sky is always blue, the birds are always singing, and her children and grandchildren are always close by.

www.ingramcontent.com/pod-product-compliance
Lightning Source LLC
LaVergne TN
LVHW041515070426
835507LV00012B/1583